Poet

Reflections on the Big House, the Death House, and the American Way of Justice

Poems by

Robert Johnson

Illustrations

Eleanor Potter
&
Jennifer Leigh Adger

Cover

Amy Hendrick

Northwoods Press : **Thomaston, Maine**

ISBN: 0-89002-367-0

Poetry // $18.95

This book is dedicated to my mother, Catherine Johnson, whose settled and secure retirement, after a life of much work and little money, is a benign case of poetic justice. In the end, she got the good life she deserved.

University Press Division
Northwoods Press, the Poet's Press
PO Box 298
Thomaston, Maine 04861

Acknowledgments

The System, from **The Collected Poems** by Stanley Kunitz. Copyright © 2000 by Stanley Kunitz. Ued by permission of W. W. Norton & Company, Inc.

Some of these poems have appeared in the following publications, to whose editors grateful acknowledgment is made: ***American Review, Black Bear Review, Tacenda, Pleasant Living Magazine***, and ***The National Catholic Reporter***.

I offer special thanks to Penny Lynn Dunn, fellow poet and editor of ***Tacenda***. Her enthusiasm for my work has been a source of inspiration. I also extend my thanks to Denise DeVries, poet and novelist. My thanks, finally, to my dedicated critics, who would drop everything and read a poem at a moment's notice: my wife, Deirdra McLaughlin, my friend, Brigid Moore, my assistant, Roxana Nabavian, and my students, notably Amanda Parker and Allison Hastings.

Other Books by Robert Johnson

Social Science

Culture and Crisis in Confinement

Condemned to Die

Hard Time

Death Work

Edited Volumes

The Pains of Imprisonment (with Hans Toch)

Crime and Punishment (with Hans Toch)

A Life for a Life (with Thomas Bernard)

Life without Parole (with Thomas Bernard)

Contents

I
Perspective

II
Crime and Punishment

III
Prison

IV
Prejudice

V
The Corporate Book of Criminal Prayer

VI
Execution

VII
Carnage and Consequences

VIII
A Closing Thought

Addendum
Domestic Justice

About the Author and Artists

That pack of scoundrels
tumbling through the gate
emerges
as the Order of the State.

The System
Stanley Kunitz
Poetic Laureate of the United States, 2000-2001

I. Perspective

Poetic Justice

Build prisons
not day-care
Lock 'em up
What do we care?

Hire cops, not counselors
Staff courts, not clinics
Wage warfare
Not welfare

Invest in felons
Ripen 'em like melons
Eat 'em raw, then
Ask for more

More poverty
More crime

More men in prison
More fear in the street

More ex-cons among us
Poetic justice

Miss Captivity

Beauty is in the eye of the beholder, and
in the hearts and minds of many we hold
behind bars.

A prison beauty contest in far-off Lithuania,
aired on local television to rave reviews,
showcased skin-deep loveliness and soul-full talent
among the female felon finalists, variously
clad in evening gowns and lingerie,
singing, dancing and reciting verse to the
cameras, amid the gracious, even effusive
applause of their captive sisters, who filled the
newly tarted up auditorium with warmth.

It was a chance to "feel ourselves women,"
said one contestant, to feel worthy of
admiration, respect, a longing glance
maybe, one day, a second chance.

If a rose blooms in captivity
Is it any less beautiful?
any less a flower?

Rightfully proud, Miss Captivity
Might one day say out loud,
I was once confined
and now I'm free.
Look at me.
A woman
Nothing more
Nothing less

On the world stage, America
Herself is Miss Captivity, Reigning
Queen of Confinement
Her Statue of Liberty
Tarnished, aging, fading
Her face stern, unforgiving
Her huddled masses

Tired and poor, now
Tempest-tossed to prison's shore
Exiled to run-on sentences
penned in permanent ink
and deadly injections
so many clinical cruxificions
all tragic defections
from the land of the free,
of debts paid and accounts cleared
of new starts and old fears
laid to rest.
Nothing more
Nothing less

Jennifer Leigh Adger

II. Crime and Punishment

Police line: Do not cross

Bright yellow bands
bind the black night
corralling chaos
containing confusion
communicating in cold chorus

Caution, stand back, stay clear
something terrible has happened here

Lights, sirens, suits
action, but too little,
too late
too bad.

Lines have been crossed
lives have been lost
long before the police
were called to the scene.

It'll take more than tape
to staunch the blood
bind the wounds
make us whole
when we can't
police ourselves.

Busted

Busted, sittin' in a squad car
knowin' you're gonna go far.

> In a manner of speaking,
> this wasn't the life you were seeking.

You thought you'd make a big score
Now you face the prison door

> held wide open,
> just for you
> by the men & women in blue.

In a split second
your life was
split in two.
You'll never be one again,
never be just you.

> You're the person you knew
> and a criminal, too. Down the road,
> even you will confuse the two.

Maybe you're not a big offender
maybe not a bad one, either.
Only time will tell.
But once we tag you a criminal
we hate to let you go.

> So this much you *do* know:
> Nothing will ever be the same.
> Your world moves in slow mo'
> it unfolds in a different frame.

Busted, sitting in a squad car
hands cuffed tight, wrists red and lined,
looking in the rearview mirror
at the life you left behind.

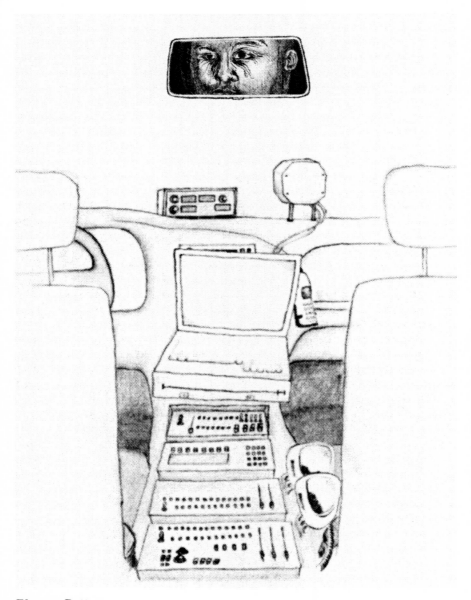

Eleanor Potter

Come as you are

Come as you are
Our place ain't far
We'll take you
in our squad car

Black and white
Lights flashing
Sirens blaring

We'll wake up the night
Shake up the 'hood
Something's not right
Now we know you're no good

What did you do?
In your boxers and tee
In your ratty slippers and messy 'do
In that face so flushed and puffy
Maybe tear-stained, too

Did you beat your wife?
Take a life?
Break and enter?
Assault with a knife?

Truth to tell
You look guilty as hell
Get an attorney,
it'll be a long journey

Cold

There's King Kong,
big and ugly
&
King Con,
big and bad.

Then there's me
I'm the one
Son of Kong
Son of Con
Son of a Gun

Number One

Big, ugly, bad
maybe a little
mad

I come first
second
third

You don't count
take my word

A cold way to
live
Only way I know to
live

'Cause I don't give
a damn
or
an inch

Colder

An orphaned, motherless child can grow up to be one cold son of a bitch, doomed from birth, disconnected, infected with a cancerous rage that eats him up, then spits us out, hurt and bleeding, maybe dead. There's no 'over the rainbow' for this guy, just one long storm. He lives for revenge -- cold world, cold comfort. Every now and again he feels a spark of empathy, like a robot, his circuits misfire, he moves jerkily, almost pausing, then forges ahead. "This is a person, this is wrong. But I'm here now, let's just get it done…"

One cold customer laid his victim out with a blast from a shotgun, the man's own shotgun, as it happens. "Watch out," the soon-to-be-dead man said, "it's loaded." Watch out. Watch me die. He crumpled to the floor, dropped like a puppet on a string, cut down with one swipe. The puppet-man looked up, and with eyes wide said, "Why have you done this to me?" That's what the killer saw in his victim's eyes. "Why have you done this to me?" Robot-man paused, circuits shorting, but only for an instant. "This didn't deter me from the task at hand. I shot him in the chest, finishing him off."

Note: Quotations drawn from a convicted murderer, since executed.

Coldest

I can take or leave executions. It's not a job I like or dislike. It's a job I've been asked to do. I try to go about every job in the most professional manner I can. If they would stop the death penalty, it wouldn't bother me. If we had ten executions tomorrow, it wouldn't bother me. I would condition my mind to get me through it.

Note: Words of an Execution Team Officer.

The problem with criminals

We hate criminals
for the harm they do
We love victims
for the hurt they go through

We love criminals
for their rebel ways
We hate victims
for their fearful gaze

Lines here are rarely clear
bruised and blurred by hate and fear
yet every day made neat and plain
by Lady Justice, in blindfold and train

Hungry for Justice

Suspects are caught, contained
questioned, interrogated,
derogated;
simmered 'til sufficiently
tender,
ready to serve
time
or have their goose
cooked
moved from frying pan to
fire
seared in the hot
seat
or chilled on a cold
gurney

Guilty as Charged...

There are no atheists on the battlefield
Where death looms
Nor innocents in the court room
Where convictions bloom

That's the presumption
Though we lack the gumption
To admit it straight out.

By the time you get to Court,
No one thinks you're innocent.
No one. Not really, anyway.
Even your mother has her doubts.

You're dirty, manhandled from day one,
Greasy prints and donut crumbs all over you.
Pushed around, head bent
Kept at arm's length
Cruisin' for a bruisin'
Down for the count.

Cops sniff you out,
paw you around
leave you dazed and numb,
ready for the DAs
the big cats these days,
who direct your sorry ass
to court that fateful day
your corpus (read carcass)
dragged and gagged
(sometimes literally)
before a judge
on high
a robed figure with a big gavel,
an ancient artifact,
polished but pointless
since His Honor is flanked
by officers with modern guns
and presides over a silent line
of humbled humanity,

fresh from cramped cages,
Unkempt, unrested, uneasy
even queasy
Compliant to a fault

They've been prepped
Marshals know where they live

The judge calls all the shots
Bang, Bang
Order in the Court!
By Order of the Most Honorable Court!
Everyone else goes through the motions
when you get right down to it,
Following his script

'"All Rise," shouts the Bailiff,
Often old and thin,
He might as well say,
"Let the Battle Begin"
and under his breath,
"We're eager to fight
'cause we almost always win."

You, hunched down,
Under a cloud of suspicion,
On the defensive, not called
defendant for nothing,
Relying for your freedom
maybe your life
On a Defense Attorney,
A Public Defender, most often,
Guardian of the poor public,
Green folk who fend off, as best they can,
the formidable forces of justice,
secure in the deep pockets of Uncle Sam

This is a trial alright, a crucible, a test,
featuring, if you raise your hand
and take the stand,
a cross examination – you,
At the left hand of the father

clearly on the outs,
Hammered by the prosecutor
questioned coldly, crossly
Handled crossly, coldly
fixed in place
for all to see.

Your life an open book,
suspended, spread-eagled
exposed

People figure, "God knows,
We'd never crucify an innocent man"

It started at the beginning,
when you talked to the detective
"Just tell your story," his gentle directive,
like he wants to hear a bedtime tale
after a long day putting people in jail.
But he didn't say, "It will be lights out for you,"
when he offered soft drinks, coffee, gum to chew.
Snack-and-chat hour though
he served the DA none other than you.

Hungrily, she ground your words,
Now called a confession, into nugget-sized
lumps of culpability, easily digested,
fast food for judge and jury
Who select a sentence
From a list of approved options

      Read carefully, as
      The menu has changed.

Settling on an American Standard:
Shake, bake, and serve time.
Easy as apple pie

Court is a world of words.
Words rule, talk counts.
'I withdraw the question,'
an attorney might say

Puff, it's gone.
'Ignore that comment,'
Voila. Never happened!
The judge intones,
In basso falsetto
'The jury is to disregard...'
Disregard what?
A bell that rang?
The latest harangue?
The whole panoply of power
paraded before them?

It's like magic,
Black Magic,
engrossing
even entertaining
in a dark way,
A juridical Disney Land
a modern wonder
Unless you're the one
Nailed on cross,
Desperately seeking
Redemption.

Her Honor

Each day at nine a.m. sharp,
Justice calls and she answers
Slipping into her chambers
Slipping out of her print dress
Into her black robes
Trading high heels
For sensible pumps
Her judicial attire
Sober, authoritative
Her I'm-always-right getup
Of this she never tires
Though some days the robes hang heavy
Cloth wearing thin in spots.

Pomp and Circumstance, she knows
Redolent of Raw Power,
Purvey a Palpable
Presumption of Prescience

Judge not, warns the Bible
But she does, and is not
Judged in turn

Much like Royalty
Who held Court
In Times Past

Much like Superman
Court of Last Resort
Another Caped Crusader

To err is human, she knows
To forgive, divine.
She makes mistakes
maybe noted on appeal,
never noted in court but
She never forgives
Never forgets

You're guilty

Or not guilty
Never innocent

Enter her world, you're tainted
Never again clean

She lives with that
You live with that
We all live with that

Uneasily, one can only hope

I Witness

An eye witness
is really an I witness.

Who we are, how we feel
shapes what we see.
Who we become
shapes what we saw

This see-saw is a
balancing act beyond
any scale of justice

Yet when we say,
"He's the one"
Our pointed finger's
As deadly as a gun

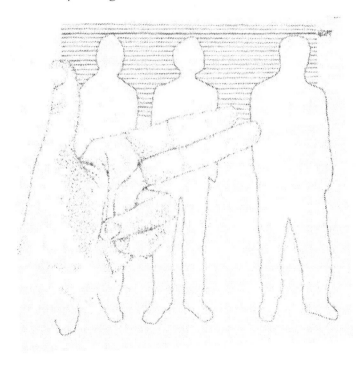

Eleanor Potter

Reasonable Doubt

"Guilty beyond a reasonable doubt"
we intone, a bit smugly, doubting
we know what's reasonable
about reasonable doubt.

Beyond a shadow of a doubt?
Dubious, I'd say, that the sun
shines that directly each day
on us, mere mortals at play
in the game of justice.

Beyond a nagging doubt, like a
stain that won't wash out or go away?
Possible, okay, but too easy
to make the culprit go away
and with him our doubts allay.

What doubt is unreasonable
for reasonable women and men
judging those who offend?

What reasonable person
has no doubts
in human affairs?

We can arrest and detain
judge and inflict pain
again and again
and be legally right
but dead wrong
without a doubt.

Justice Shoppers

Some prosecutors are eager justice shoppers,
Charging everything in sight
Up and down the aisles
Copping one special or another
Scoring one bargain then another
Living for the deals and discounts
Rung up every working day
Ca-ching, Ca-ching.

It's an addiction
each sentence
pure satisfaction

The cart may be overflowing
Filled with bargains we can't afford.
But tell that to the DA.
Tab don't go his way
Today or any day.
Only we pay.

Barely Burglary

He didn't mean it,
said his lawyer,
Had he seen it

> the big black & white
> wailing siren & blinking light

He would've kept on walking
that dark & rainy night

A lame defense
proffered professionally
Barely believable
An offense
in its own
Rite.

Super Juror

Up in the court house –
Is it a bird, is it a plane!
No, It's Super Juror!

Foe of DAs everywhere,
faster off the topic than a
speeding train of thought
able to distort tall arguments
with a single leap of faith
Super Juror metes out justice
on his own terms.

Like Clark Kent, these closet heroes
dress like you or me, but when the chips are down,
they fly off to handle the world's problems
convicting and exonerating
as the shifting winds move them
imaginary capes and all
on rising thermals
and sinking depressions
eager, but unsteady,
a fickle force
in the fight
for justice

Note: The term "super juror" is used regularly and derisively by some prosecutors.

Criminal Justice

To be a criminal is inimical
to your health and well being
or to your being at all.

Crime pays, sure, but
the hours are long
good help is hard to find
and the work can kill you.

Plus we capture most criminals,
then cage them,
first in holes, now in cells.

Some prisoners we flat-out shoot –
in the old days, with any weapon that came to hand
nowadays with lethal drugs.
Ain't progress grand?

We've come a long way, I suppose
but a cell's not a home and
dead is dead.

It's criminal, what we do to criminals,
and what criminals do to us.
That's where we get the criminal
in criminal justice.

So where's the justice?

Loss

Like so many before me,
I take the stand
solemnly, to swear
on my broken life,
my face ashen,
bloated by grief
my legs moving slowly,
awkwardly,
my head in a fog
the pain palpable
even now, more than
a year later.

My son is dead,
I am dead.
Life goes on
without us.

His killer sits
before me, in
shackles and khakis
very much alive.
He may one day walk free.

Not me, imprisoned for life,
My world shrunk to a
grave and a bedroom
one tended
one untouched
both washed
by a river of tears

My life hangs by a
thread, sewn in sedatives
numb, desolate
beyond redemption.

Why go on
without my son

my light
the one
I rose for
each day?

Make his killer's
punishment
a monument
to my loss.

Leave *his* father a
grave and a bedroom
one tended
one untouched
both washed
by a river of tears,
his life hanging by
a chemical thread
numb, desolate
as good as dead.

Justice.
Not just us.
Anyone.
Everyone.

An eye for an eye
A blind animal cry
Raw revenge

Name Game

They bought your drugs
You sold your life
They made you an offer
you couldn't refuse.
Now you're facing

Five to ten
Ten to life
Life with an out
Life without
Death on a gurney
the ultimate clout

The ball's in your court
to your own self be true
Rat someone out
get less time to do.
Guilty or not, most
any name will do

Five to ten
Ten to life
Life with an out
Life without
Death on a gurney
the ultimate clout

They all play the same game
the criminal name game
cops and thugs in the same frame

That's how we fill our prisons
one rat at a time, on
each side of line.

Life Sentences

The judge gave him life, we say
with no sense of the irony

      or the arrogance
      or the enormity

of sentences given out every day
in court rooms across the nation.

God gave him life.
His mother gave him life.

The judge takes life, condemning
people to cells or coffins
which are pretty much the same
thing, when you think about it.

Testilying

White lies
Convicting
Bad Guys

Sending
Sacrifice Flies

To the Prison Wall

*Note: Seasoned defense attorneys often refer to police testimony in
criminal cases as testilying, or routine lying in the course of testimony.*

Demons One and All

At the bar of justice
Innocence is no bar to
Conviction
Confinement
Condemnation
Consignment
to the junkyard of lost souls.

After the fall
we brand criminals
demons one and all
once and for all

Innocent? Too late,
Too good to be true
A technicality, not fate
Not the real you.

We swallow our mistakes,
keep them safe and warm
in the belly of the beast
where they belong.

III. Prison

A Zoo Near You

A decent zoo captures
in miniature, the
natural environs of the
animals within.

Prisons don't capture
the free world of the
ranging felon

They turn their world
upside down and
inside out.

If prisons were more like zoos
maybe we'd visit them
and share our families
and our food
with the captives.

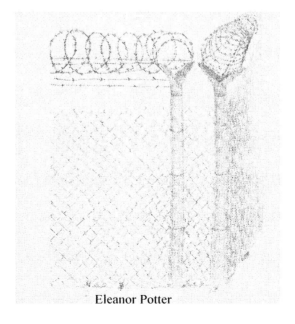

Eleanor Potter

American Dream House

Ah, the American Big House
Country Club Confinement, Catering
to the Cloistered Criminal Class,
Perennial thorn in the side of those
who bitterly begrudge the lowly felon
his meager lot, really no more than
three hots and a cot.

Oh, thinks the angry person on the street,
To retire at government expense, to be
bound by golden handcuffs and
escorted to gilded cages, to have
meals served daily by a
trained, uniformed staff!

Give me prison any day,
such folk are wont to say.
Lifers have the life!
No work, no wife
no bills to pay!

Next thing you know, our
pouting purveyors of punishment
will pose for pictures, proudly,
with the Lock Ness Monster.*

Like that mythical beast,
palatial prisons and
carefree convicts are
creatures not found
in any nation
other than our
imagination.

Note: The Loch Ness Monster is not locked up, except in this poem.

Hot House

Prison is the endless summer
of a convict's discontent,
shadeless, hot, unforgiving.

This Big House
This Hot House is
Their House for
Better and Worse

Criminals boil with
passion, escaping like
steam, but only from
frying pan to fire.

They come ready for the heat
grilled by cops to a turn,
some with a third degree burn

A few feral flowers bloom
in our Big Hot Houses,
out of sheer conviction.

Most wilt, hanging limp
like so many dangling
sentences.

Prison

Prison
life poisoning
punishment
for people of poverty

Prison
lash of rebuke
wielded like a whip
on the working wounded

Prison
dark black
dungeon of despair
denizen of the dispossessed

Prison
waste dump
for wasted lives,
house of refuge
for human refuse,
warehouse for
worn out,
used up
cast off
careworn creatures
now humbled and discarded.

Prison
time out
of sight,
time out
of mind,
for those
who don't
toe the line.

One Uniformed Woman

In the penitentiary,
she'd tamed lions
without a whip
without a weapon.

She'd whistle,
iron doors rolled
back, out came
the big cats
one per cage
cool, calm, collected
lined up, in a row.

A great show,
Greatest show on earth
One uniformed woman
starched collar, sensible shoes
in the center ring.

At the supermax,
prison of prisons
she's the tame one,
sliding steamy styrofoam
boxes, filled with chow
into each cell
through a slot.

Work's hot
collars wrinkle
feet sag
days drag

"Slide the tray
stay out the way"
that's her day.

Cats stay confined
Lion tamer's resigned
Nothing but hard time.

Nothing super
About supermax
putting guards
in prison.

Mistress of the Cell Block

She stoops to conquer
slowly removing his jump suit
jumping him in his cell
No concern for dirt or smell
or who might tell

A moment free of hell
is what drives him
to her

She risks it all, but
men on their knees, please
it's hard to resist
She's on a roll
in control

Gender bends prison bars
with bare female bodies
launching men into space
Venus in orbit, Mars rising, a
miracle of modern punishment

Sex in prison, with men
who've been around the block
And women who feel free to

Knock on any cell
any cell at all
risking it all
For love
in a cold climate.

*Note: In some prisons, sex between female officers and male in-
mates, technically a case of rape, is believed to be more common
than inmate-on- inmate rape.*

Master of the Messhall

He strides imperiously to the serving line,
his serving line, a baton in his ham-sized
hand, tapping it lightly against his leg,
twisting it slightly, with a hint of menace.

"The chow stops here,"
he says with a sneer,
a big man in a
small job, always
a bad situation.

He talks in clipped phrases,
Terse
Tough
Staccato
Bravado

"Easy on the mash, my man"
he says to a server
who knows the routine
but tests him anyway

"Hand back that snack, Jack"
he says to a con
who growls
lifts a leg
moves on.

"Easy on the steak, Jake"
another server busted
bold as a brass monkey
adjusting his plastic hair net
shamelessly, like nothing
happened.

"Put down the juice, Bruce"
You've got too much meat to eat
Too much garden in your salad
Too much starch for your march

He's got it goin' on now, talkin'
Smooth as butter, moving
Slow as molasses
Takin' names and
Kickin' asses.

"This is a prison, mister"
He says to no one in particular.
"If you can't take the heat
Stay offa my beat."

Only he knows
how thin the veneer
how fragile the façade
that gets him through each day

Petty ain't pretty
but order matters

Let down your guard
and some cons will
Eat you alive

A Cell with a View

Shadowy forms mill about aimlessly
oblivious to the stone walls
and razor wire fences
that surround and contain them
like so many cattle at a slaughter house.

A whistle blows, ending their fragile freedom.
"The Yard is Clooooosed"
bellows a deep baritone voice.
The words hang in space, then echo
down the concrete canyons of the prison yard.

Herded up and moved out,
led shuffling and murmuring
through cramped corridors
to claustrophobic cages,
their bodies branded by
jagged shards of light from
flickering flourescent tubes
perched menacingly overhead.

Sun light at dusk makes
a forced entry into the cell block,
cutting through motes of dust
like a sharp knife through tender flesh.

Echoes of cell doors closing,
steel on steel, hard, final
rise to greet the dying light of day,
filtering down rows of cells
stacked neatly like boxes,
but no ribbons or bows,
no prizes or surprises
for the men inside.

A prisoner peers through plexiglass partitions
like an old man with cataracts, his vision
blurred by a waterfall of air holes,
ragged and rough edged,

so many bullet wounds
from a drive-by shooting of the soul.

There by popular demand, each convict
will be held for a long engagement,
sometimes with a few intermissions,
in the theater of wasted lives
we call The Big House, home to the
double-feature creature-classic:
the punishment of crime and
the crime of punishment.

Reptile House

Men lie like snakes
coiled tight in bright,
shadeless, barbed-wire run
shedding shirts
seeking shelter
under searing sun

Soon, too soon
called, culled
carried along
colorless corridors to
cloistered cells, cold
cement crevices
dark and dank
close and musky

Readily, too readily
slouching, stretching
sliding along
slow, servile
syrupy
like warm spit
oozing lazily into
wide jawed
empty bellied
cages

Easily, too easily
flesh tears
souls sunder on
serrated steel bars
industrial strength
teeth, grinding
swallowing, storing
small sacrifices
in the belly of the beast

Late, too late
animation suspended

pain unended
      palpable, pervasive, perpetual, the
      perennial price of punishment

Prison primordial
time immemorial.
The fit may survive
but no one comes out
fully alive.

Signs and Portends from Planet Prison

"All illiterate inmates line up here,"
read the sign on the prison wall.

Another sign warned, "this institution is reserved
for the most dangerous, disruptive and diverse inmates."
Reserved? Diverse inmates?
Has political correctness come to this?

At a women's prison, a sign advertises a long running program:
"Girl Scouts Behind Bars." As with Prince Albert in a Can,
one can only think, "Please, let them out!"

Female visitors to a supermax prison,
are greeted by a sign telling them they may
"only wear skirts of a modest length,"
which in a kind world would mean topless women
in insubstantial, nominal or even skimpy dresses.
After all, hard-core prisoners don't get to see many women.

The other day, after a session in prison,
I stopped for lunch at a Wendy's restaurant.
The sign outside read, "hiring losers."
In bold letters, no less.
Closers might be losers, by some reckonings,
but why rub it in?

The problem, I realized, is bigger than prison,
but perhaps most painful in prison.

"What we have here is a failure to communicate."

That's today's Gospel,
According to Luke,
Cool Hand Luke

More from Planet Prison

The inmate refused to "'bend and spread 'em'," saying,
"I've never showed my ass to nobody and I ain't starting now."
He was duly reprimanded by Officer Chippendale.

The mail order form in the prisoner's file read:
"Stocking hat, ski mask, ear plugs. Rush shipment."
The order was processed promptly.

Notation in a prisoner's file, complete and unabridged:
"Parole denied, rehear in 10 years."

Notation in a prisoner's file, under Demographics:
"Dark" "Large" "Christian" "Carpenter"

Penal Envy

People the world over criticize America's prisons, calling them
dreadful, dreary, degrading even deadly dungeons.
True, but we know the root of the problem:
Penal Envy.

Our prisons are big and solid, remarkable erections, built to
last. We get new ones up fast, thanks to private industry,
whose unctuous pitch has gotten us all thoroughly
Aroused.

Full beyond our wildest, most lurid dreams, our prisons
hold two million caged captives and counting;
even the Russians and Chinese can't
Keep Up.

The Joint, the Big House, the Rock – by any measure
the manly pride of our punishment system, our
prisons are engorged to the point of
Tumescence.

Our sentences are stiff and long, rigid and unyielding,
the prospect of release a heady fantasy, a tease;
Our convicts are lean and mean, solid and
muscular, bare-chested and tattooed,
hard men made harder by
Hard Time.

It's a sore point, but size matters in matters penal.
We may spare the rod, but when it
comes to prison, we don't
Dick Around.

Hard Time

I chill out
in cold storage
concrete and steel
my constant companions

My life a
closed cage
suppressed rage
servile submission
sheer survival

On good days.

Echoes of present and past
things done that can't be undone
bells rung that can't be unrung
swirl in and around me
oceans of regret that
surround me, drown me
'Til I surrender

Every night.

I do time
Time does me
I'm a prisoner
Never free
Ever.

Rock Pile

On a good day
she dig gems
from the rock pile
of her imagination

Sifting
dirt and dust
for a nugget
of truth

for a diamond
in the rough
for a glimmer of hope
in the hell she calls
home.

Light from Another Country

Knife bright light
fills up the cell, rays
Bouncing off gray cement walls
piercing his eyes, slicing
through lids squeezed

Tight against the
Dark night of despair
The hard light of introspection

Revealing who he is,
Where he is,
What he will become

In time, a creature of the night
On the wrong side of right
He knows this, we know this
It's as clear as the light
Of day.

Risen from Prison

Risen from prison
back from the dead
released convicts
rejoin the living.

Alleluia! Alleluia!
They have returned!
It is a miracle!

Every day
A Miracle

Our prodigal sons
and daughters
return
every day,

From graveyards
we call prisons,

Each release
a resurrection
a quest for
grace,

For life
to begin
anew

Amen.

IV. Prejudice

Discrimination

Discrimination,
the leading edge of
       oppression
makes a deep and lasting
       impression
on folk we offer no
       concession
yet find in most any
       expression
a cause for righteous
       repression
'cause they don't look like
       you or me.

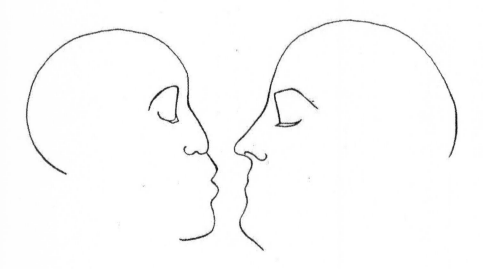

Eleanor Potter

Faggot

Faggot: a bundle of sticks,
ready for burning.
Few people know that.
Most people think,
Faggot: a low-life homosexual,
a walking piece of shit,
ready for burning.

Or at least suitable
for daily humiliation
with words that
bind and sear
the soul.

Can anyone be gay
in a world like ours?

Feeding Friendly

You can learn your colors
at our bird feeder
a font of
aviary diversity.

Red Birds, Black Birds,
Blue and Yellow Birds
Birds of all colors
flock together
at our feeder.

Peacefully.

There are squabbles, sure
but things get worked out.
This isn't rocket science.
A bird brain is
all it takes.

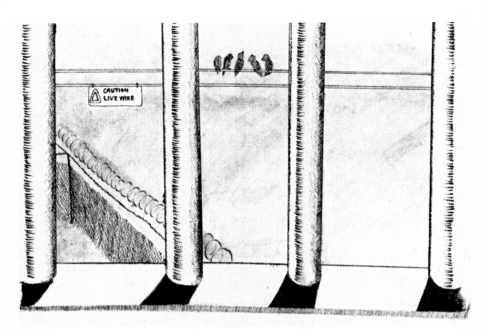

Eleanor Potter

Black Birds

Five and twenty black birds
all in a row
toe to toe
nowhere to go

Five and twenty black cons
all in a row
cell to cell
nothing to tell

The story is told
They won't grow old
For by and by
Each must fly

To that death house
in the sky.

Our Black Prison Nation

At first blush, today's black prisons
look like a green wound, a fresh assault,
something new under the sun.

But Old Hannah* burns hot and relentless
on peoples pushed to the margins,
exposed, defenseless.

This modern conflagration is but a recapitulation
of patterns dating back to our country's creation
seen all too clearly in slave ship and plantation
in share cropper hut and urban underclass station
reaching full flower in our black prison nation.

A world apart, so black, so rife with misery
the prison is utterly foreign to those who be
wealthy, especially white and wealthy,
those paragons of privilege given a healthy
dose of justice in the land of the free

So it is, as ever, a given:
The rich get richer
and the poor get prison.
Especially in the slums
where color is life's prism.

A lucky few from penal interment
come risen (after three decades, not three days)
but they, unlike Christ
are unbidden
and unwelcome
in the land where only
         the white
                  and wealthy
                           are truly free.

*Note: Old Hannah is a name for the sun found in slave and plantation
prison songs.*

I want to say this about my state: When Strom Thurmond ran for president, we voted for him. We're proud of it. And if the rest of the country had followed our lead, we wouldn't have had all these problems over all these years, either."

– Trent Lott
at Strom Thurmond's
100th birthday party

A Lott to Learn

We have a lott to learn
from our Republican leaders,
'specially the one's who've missed
the 21th century and stayed in Ole Miss,
circa nineteen hundred and forty eight
when everything was black and white
and white was right
and black stayed back
at the end of the line
on chain gang time
when things were fine
in the good ole days
those lazy, crazy, racist days
when lynching was all the rage
and white women wore chantilly lace
and rap was a sheet for those black of face
and white sheets were fashionable attire
for men on horseback lighting crosses afire
Oh, those were the days
days we miss a lot
according to Senator Lott
and folks who, admit it or not,
feel a lot
like him.

V. The Corporate Book of Criminal Prayer

Psalm of Wonder

The world is
my oyster,
I shall not
want.

I lay me down
with fine jobs
and wealth to
flaunt.

It pays
to have friends
in high
places.

A Patriarch's Protocol

Our Father
who art in
Headquarters
Hollow be
Thy Claim
Thy Fortune Come
Thy Will be Mum
On CNN
and before
Congress.
Lead us Not
Into our Prison Nation
And Deliver us
From Civil Obligation
to our Fellow Man

Amen

Tithing
"Take the Money and Run"

Witness Enron's end run
to infamy
in which fat cats
played investors
like a symphony
and employees
like a cheap video game.

Bush-league stuff
even if Bush
and crew
are clean.

Eleanor Potter

In the Beginning

We were cannibals once
and hungry
feeding freely
on the flesh
of our enemies.

War was a long buffet line,
at least some of the time,
in early times,
perhaps more times
than we care to admit or remember.

Sidling up to the salad bar of vanquished foes
we'd pick and choose from the
carnal bounty of killing fields.

Portions of War – Big servings, many choices,
A loin here, a second joint there,
A little brain on the side, always a delicacy.

More victories, more bodies,
more selections, more consumption.
Winners grow fat on the fat of losers,
sucked lovingly from warm, sliced bones.

Eat fast, eat fat, get fat, live large.
It's an old story, maybe the oldest.
To the victor belong the spoils,
eaten soon after they fall, before they spoil

No treats to be had from sinew
or tendon or bone, but
Victory is always sweet,
a dessert in itself.

And then there are the women.
Kill and eat the men and children,
especially the fleshy ones;
take the women to go.

A grisly, glorious, gory,
unrestrainedly hedonistic business,
this sating of animal appetites,

Which serves as model and metaphor
for capitalism in the raw,
where the rich
kill and eat the poor

Sucking wealth from their labor
picking their tired bones clean

Living off the fat
of the toiling unseen

Until all that's left
for the hopeless bereft
are illness and early death.

Money Talks

Law
Tired old whore
Looking
For an easy score

Legal tender
Hard currency
Money talks
Nobody walks
Without it

Green
Goes free
Black & Brown
Stay down

White
Be right
Keep the bucks
In sight

No bread?
Good as dead

Law
A hard bitch
A cold lay
When you can't
Pay

*Note: An old joke about the death penalty goes like this: Only those
without capital get capital punishment.*

VI. Execution

Good People

"Good people are always so sure they're right,"
said Barbara Graham, last woman executed
by the State of California, back in '54
Immortalized by Susan Hayward in the
classic film, I Want to Live. Her last words
may be the last word on capital punishment.
Good people condemning bad people
Sure they are right, even as
Exonerations mount, even as
We lean heavily, unsteadily
on our hidden execution rite
To get us through one more dark night
And then another...

Jennifer Leigh Adger

The Iceman Killeth

The execution-style killer is a pillar
of the prison community.
Cold as ice, hard as steel,
he is admired and feared.
But he pays with his life
counted in empty years on prison tiers,
or a living death on condemned row
before, a broken man, he is taken in tow
to the death house and its chamber of fears.
      Punishment hurts

The law's executioner is a pillar
of the free community.
Cold as ice, hard as steel
he is admired and feared.
But he pays with his soul
counted in bad dreams that toll
slowly, during long sleepless nights
or in mordant cynicism, which like sin
eats at life slowly, from within.
      Punishment hurts

All of us, made
Cold as ice, hard as steel
unable to feel
the harm we do
in the name of justice.

Needle Work

Lethal Injection
a deadly intersection
in the search for perfection
in the war on crime.

      A dead criminal
      silent and still
      cradled by catheters,
      clinging to a cross.

Lethal Injection
the ultimate rejection
a poison confection
spread over the body of crime.

      Condemned criminals
      all in a row
      suitable for framing.
      Unmoving, uncomplaining.

Lethal Injection
a chemical subjection
for people of complexion
whose supine demise
lends authority to lies

Enshrined in law
beyond inspection
beneath reflection
in the search for perfection
in the war on crime.

      "They sigh and drift off to sleep," we hear.
      "Much worse for their victims," we're told is clear.
      "Really nothing to fear," we all exclaim.
      How can anyone protest or complain,
      in the face justice so tame,
      so transparently humane.

Execution day, we pray
brings sweet, sound slumber.
Free of guilt or remorse or regret
we feel sure the number
put to death on prison gurneys
take their final journeys
decently, justly
as if by personal election
in the search for perfection
in the war on crime.

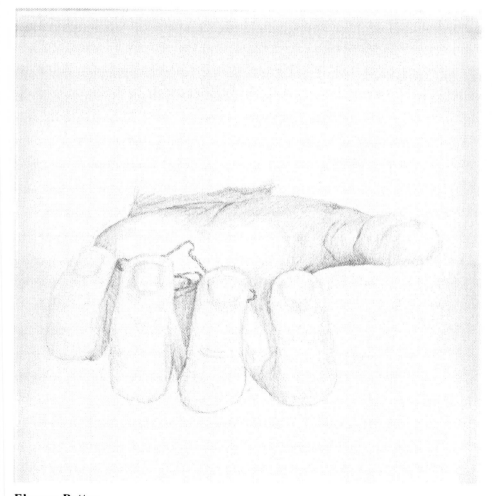

Eleanor Potter

Execution Night

My son was born in the morning, only days before the execution.
I was there, amid the
blood and the gore, and
the tears of joy.
He cried, I cried, and
the world opened before him.

The condemned man was killed as midnight approached.
I was there, amid the
burned flesh and the yawning, gaping mouth, and
the vacant eyes.
He died, no one cried, and
the world closed around him.

I couldn't help but think of them
together
dearly arrived, dreadfully departed
bookends, brackets
around the day
around existence

This man before me,
shaved down to his tender skin
an overgrown baby, really

      swaddled in denim
      strapped to the chair

delivered unto death
in our name.

Alien Justice

Raise your space helmet visor
if you think Sigourney Weaver is God.
Okay, check your air supply first.

Alexander Williams, a
Georgia death row inmate
thinks Sigourney Weaver is God.
Does that mean he's crazy?
Officials thought so, and
stayed his execution.

Sigourney Weaver may not be God
nor even a mere Goddess
but she is a force to be reckoned with.

Not a Dark Force
or an Alien Force
or even a Moving Part on an Axis of Evil.

She is, instead, a Wonder Woman
as we have come to know Her
after Women's Liberation
unchained our Sisters
and let them reach for the Stars
and maybe a distant Galaxy or two.

Thanks, Sigourney
God knows we needed you.
And if you can save just one death row inmate,
so much the better.

Note: Williams subsequently had his sentence commuted.
He's been granted life. Ms. Weaver had no comment.
None was needed.

burnt offerings

there
in the damp basement
of the aging prison
near the
chair

death
the scent of
burnt offerings
hangs in the
air

a
devil's brew of
mildew, flesh, and
fear

the
chair is gone
(the latest reform)
the smell lives
on

A Messy Business

Justice can be a messy business.
We used to torture criminals on the rack
then kill them. To call that justice was a stretch,
but we did, turning levers with abandon.
All righty tighty, no lefty loosey, until the poor wretches
were pulled nearly apart, gaining a few inches
in height, but of course it was excruciating to move
even a little, and impossible to walk. So criminals
weren't taller, they were longer.
Sometimes we'd beat these long-fellows
to the point of death and then
tear them limb from limb
with the help of horses or
men with horse sense and little more.

All this was bloody
and the screams terrible,
even to medieval ears,
but it was great community fun.
We saw the Devil among us
and we had Him on the run.
Villages would fight for the right
to punish, pushing and pulling
and spitting, even biting
in a preview of tortures to come.
And we think television is violent!

Things are more clinical today,
tame as a housebroken dog.
True, there's still a hanging or two,
an occasional firing squad at dawn,
a fair number of electrocutions
though seating is limited, what with
modern sensibilities holding us back.
Today's executions are bloodless,
Victims quiet and still. No one
on the rack was quiet and still.
And then there were the cheers
The crowds eager for souvenirs.

Today we doubt the Devil, so
our criminals are small letter types,
as in bad or evil, or even monster
not Dark Demon or Minion of Satan.
If crime has lost it drama, so has punishment.
We rely on lethal injection in most cases.
No one knows what it's like, of course,
but no one ever does with execution.
Or cares. All these changes in methods
were for me and you, the viewing public.
We used to like blood and gore,
and screaming in stereo, so
stones and clubs, swords and fire
worked just fine. Now we want
a tame death scene,
a tableau of criminals
looking alive but dead
like people well waked.
"He never looked better," we might say
of the average dead man walking.
Maybe people do say that.
I'm sure they think it. Especially
when they think of the victim, who,
in timeless fashion, dies screaming
amid blood, sweat and tears
awash in pools of feces and urine and vomit.

The image of condemned criminals
in peaceful, waxy repose is the
real appeal of lethal injection.
A pinprick, maybe a gasp for air
but never a mark on them.
No surface blemishes; no signs of pain.
We want death domesticated, emasculated
so lethal injection is the ticket.

But what next? Whither the technology
of state-made death?
We could use lasers, but someone would
have to point the beam. Looks wild, aggressive,
implicates us in an act of violence. God forbid

we should kill people and feel
implicated in an act of violence.

One candidate: the ubiquitous microwave.
We hesitate, understandably, feeling squeamish.
There is the nasty association with ovens,
which brings to mind the Nazis
and their primitive ovens, but we did
use gas for a spell, and we put offenders
in capsules not all that different from ovens,
so we can get over this.
You don't see human rights activists
shunning the microwave, do you?
They zap their food as often as regular folk, maybe more,
since they have to be out all day protesting injustice
while the rest of us can go home and watch TV,
letting our food simmer over a real flame,
stirring during commercials.

The beauty of execution by microwave is that
it's a clean, quiet killer – it cooks the life out of you
without doing any visible damage to the body,
at least that the naked eye can see, and remember,
it's only the visible body that matters. What you see
is what you get. An added bonus, justice consumers:
we can cook the condemned and eat our dinner, too,
without so much as the touch of a human hand
on the newly departed.

So I propose a small, crisp salute – a micro-wave –
to a new frontier in capital punishment.
True, we're treating felons like animals,
but they're dead meat anyway, aren't they?

Dead Letter Law

Habeas Corpus, the Great Writ
the Get-Out-of-Jail-Free bit,
If they bite, spitting up the body
slightly chewed but undigested
more or less whole.

But the Great Writ, now
thanks to Congress, really
a late writ, a writ-small
writ, hardly a writ-at-all writ.

Habeas is a corpse, man,
so much dead letter law,
at least in capital cases.
You get the body back
in a box or a bag
death the only release.

Un-appealing, but that's how
Capital appeals go these days.
'Cause we're terror crazy
and too scared or lazy
or maybe just too hasty
to see the nasty chalk outline
drawn around the law.

Postcard from Death Row

Single room, grate view
round-the-clock room service
uniformed security staff
all utilities, medical and dental covered.

Last meal special —
open menu, all you can eat.

Wish you were here!

VII. Carnage and Consequences

Global Village Life

The image of the world as
one big Global Village
has appeal to us, folks
who've mostly never lived in a village.

Getting to know something
about everyone on the planet
sounds so connected,
so authentic.
Who could resist?

We forgot about village idiots
and about chronic malcontents
whose stupidity and bad temper
can wreak havoc on our lives.

Worse, we forgot about victims
of injustice, real and imagined,
whose resentments simmer and boil
just below the surface of village life.

And worst of all, we forgot that our Global Village
was a stepchild of technology
not the flowering of community

A place where guns and bombs
and hijacked planes
can be weapons of terror
wielded by the wounded,
who make it their life's work to
annihilate innocents at will
in numbers beyond comprehension.

Misery has always loved company.
It used to be that the miserable
had only each other's company.
Now, in our cozy Global Village,

the forlorn and the rejected
the isolate and the fanatic
see the happy, chosen peoples
at close range

Even if only on TV, radio, or Internet,
like targets in a shooting gallery
or in a video game of doom.
Some of them take aim,
and the rest is history.

Eleanor Potter

It takes a child. . .

Operation Infinite Justice
has long now winged its worrisome way
East, crossing continents and cultures
menacing peoples alien to us
and us to them.

Finite bombs have fallen,
and may yet fall, inflicting
infinite suffering
in retribution for our
infinite suffering.
Innocents perish
in punishment
for the perishing
of innocents.

War, we are told,
is the way of history
the way to Enduring Peace.
But we could rewrite history
as we enter the 21th century
waging not a war, but a crusade –
against global injustice, the
dark mother of desperate acts.

Peace means inclusion, then connection.
Inclusion makes growing fields
instead of killing fields.
Connection shores up islands of possibility
in an ocean of goodwill.
Children know these things,
learned hard but learned well
in every kindergarten and playground
on the planet.

If it takes a village to raise a decent child,
it may take a child's sense of decency
to make our world – the Global Village –
a decent place to live.

Dial nine-one-one, Believe

Nine-one-one
planes crashing into
buildings collapsing on
people on the run

> Nine-eleven
> drop to your knees,
> pray to heaven

Nine-one-one
smoke and rubble covering
molten graves fusing
flesh and steel as one

> Nine-eleven
> drop to your knees
> pray to heaven

Nine-one-one
mass murder makes
mass media makes
masses numb

> So many killed
> so many times

> So many bereft
> Is there anyone left
> untouched?

Nine-one-one
a day to remember, of
a bygone September, when
we came together as one
People.

> Nine-eleven
> drop to your knees,
> pray to heaven

Thank God
if you can still
believe.

Modern Mariners, We?

Enemies, enemies, everywhere
Nary a moment to think.

Enemies, enemies, everywhere
Oh, how the world does shrink.

Enemies, enemies, everywhere
Watch what you open, eat or drink.

Enemies, enemies, everywhere
Are we on the brink?

What Albatross did we selfishly shed
to have so many wanting us dead?

Is it our madness for modernity?
Our material immaturity?

Or our secrets, like Victoria's,
so publicly displayed?

That make us reprehensible, indefensible,
a source of endless enmity and envy
to much of the world?

Enemies, enemies, everywhere
our best hope is to persevere,
affirming values we hold dear,

Freedom in its varied forms,
some tasteful, others tasteless
all utterly delicious.

Dueling Deities

Dueling Deities
demanding discrimination
Precious Pieties
polluting proprieties

God on the end
of every sword and pen
declaiming the end
of life as we know it
for the sinner in the other
station, nation, congregation.

Damnation.
It's all the rage these days.

If zealots weren't as common as fleas
Humankind might find its ease
in one another, without theology
hiding our shared genealogy
which makes you and me, us and him
a Siamise twin, under the skin.

Jihadi Gras

Osama bin Laden came
laden with treats
Christian Kabobs, Hebrew meats
Fettuccini Al Queda
A killer feast

Hamas brought the humus
No chick peas, please
Chicks and parties
Don't mix, they believe.

Hizbollah brought baklava
Covered in balaclavas
Straight from Ramallah
What great fellahs!

A merry time was had by all
'Til Sami the suicide bomber
head wrapped too tight
burst onto the scene

"This party was the bomb,"
he'd been told, "a demented
Global Village Prom"
So he razed the roof
looking for virgins
and ultimate truth

In the aftermath
in the cold light of day, as
dreams of deliverance fade away
like smoke from burning rubble
like blood from streets awash in tears
each of us drowning in our mortal fears

We might one day say, Terrible,
But true, what we do
when we close our eyes
when we live by lies
dead certain we're right
that only our light
our religious rendition
dispels the dark night
salves the human condition

V-Days

V is for Victory
Hopes George, a
Burning Bush
Yearning to
Vanquish Evil, maybe
Vindicate Dad

V is for Villain,
Senses Saddam, a
Sad man, a Mad man,
A Force for Venality
in his Arid Principality

V is for Victim
Knows the Iraqi man on the street
Violation a way of life –
first homegrown guns and germs and strife
now foreign planes and heaps of rubble,
an endless vista of pain and trouble

V is for Valium
given to children
like candy, by
helpless parents, hoping
drugged dreams will

Cushion the Shock,
Mute the Awe, of
America's Modern war, where

Military monsters, red
in tooth and claw,
like dragons spew forth fire
hot and raw,
and with licking tongues
beckon, threaten, blacken
every door

By dark of desert days,
amid the wind- and
bomb-fed haze;
by bright of desert nights
lit by missiles in flight

A Martial Spectacular, in
Living Color and Surround Sound
Playing in the Theater of War
They call home.

Postscript

As the War Cools Down
(and Ethnic Tensions Heat Up)
V is for Vacuum,
of Power and Order,
maybe Hope

Iraq, now a Hollow Place,
Void at its Core, like the
Empty Space
Inside the
Statue of Saddam,
Pulled to the Ground,
Dragging Down
This Vacant Man, who
Brought a Kingdom
To its Knees, and
Cast a Civilization into
a Desert of Despair

Cards of Fate

The fate of Saddam & Friends
Is in the Cards
Handed out to the military
Like sports memorabilia
Each picturing a Heavy Hitter.
No season or lifetime stats,
but they're all Good at being Bad
year in, year out.

Living Free is the Best Revenge

We're asked to give up civil rights
in the fight against terrorism.
People are dying for us,
can't we make sacrifices, too?

And aren't we just facing reality?
Civil rights suit civil times,
martial rights, martial times.
Aliens and Traitors, mostly people of hue
deserve only the justice we're wont to do.

But in a free society, aren't
civil rights and human rights
one and the same,
in good times and in bad,
in war and in peace
'til death do us part?

We may stop being civil
when we're at war, but
we never stop being human.

If some of us must die for freedom,
the rest of us should live it,
every day, in every way,
we can.

A Nation of Laws?

John Adams famously said
America is a nation of laws, not men.
Trouble is, we have more laws than men,
more laws than men, women and children,
more laws, maybe, than sense.

Suspected terrorists have broken the law, we're told,
that's why hundreds are held incommunicado.
But one can hardly walk down the street
without breaking some law.

Any stroll on any block
can become a line-up,
what cops call a "perp walk."

That's not terrorism, I'll grant you,
but it is scary.

Felon du Jour

"Authorities grilled Malvo for seven hours," read the headline
about the loquacious young sniper suspect. Meanwhile,
a mute Muhammad, moody mastermind, apparent parent
marinated in his own juices, sauteeing in his solitary cell.

Fresh fish and seasoned mentor will be filleted
in due course and served to a hungry public
when the time is ripe.

*Note: Lee Boyd Malvo and John Muhammad have been arrested and
charged in the sniper case in which eleven persons were killed and two
injured in the Washington, D.C. metro area during the fall of 2002.*

One Shot Away

Left for Dead
Right for Life
Dead on Arrival
Consumed by Strife
Story of a Life

Sordid, trite, but
for the gun, the
big, long gun.

The great equalizer
The great tranquilizer
of the human conscience.

DOA
five one day
six more to pay
snipers at play

Yet two got away
reason to pray

Rest of us anxious
ducking and jiving
struggling and conniving
to get on with each day
knowing our maker's
but one shot away.

Terminator

He's a maverick moral cop
is our James Kopp
in thrall to Jesus
above it all, he takes the law
into his own hands,
hands holding high a
high powered rifle, aiming
high, chest and head
high, high on grace
high on something
hiding in plain sight
in Caesar's court,
lost in a baggy suit
a moronic smirk on
an oddly tilted head
cocked to one side
big glasses resting uneasy
on a narrow face, windows
to a narrow mind.

He stands straight when he shoots,
head oddly tilted
cocked to one side
but no smile, not yet
He's busy stalking his game
tracking them in God's name,
right to the nest, killing them
in front of their chicks, claiming to be
the best sort of Christian,
Protector of the Unborn
Terminator of Terminators
Killer for a Cause
Willing to murder
Without pause
Or compunction
Or compassion.

Moral contortion
Emotional Fervor
Choreographed Carnage
Close to home.

Note: James Kopp confessed to murdering Barnard Slepian, an obstetrician who performed abortions as part of his medical practice

September Storm

Beds of burning charcoal
pulsating, throbbing
loiter on the horizon
up to no good

Full-on storm clouds
churning, roiling
lurk overhead, riding
low over the water
thick, tufted,
puffed out, so many
dark predators
heavy with menace

Threads of mist,
fine as spun sugar,
laced across the sky
like lassos in flight,
frame the scene –

Nature's silver lining.
"This, too,
shall pass."

VIII. A Closing Thought

Beaten in Eden

Adam and Eve sinned pretty much
right out of the chute
but disobedience, deception
misappropriation of fruit?

Deviance of a menial sort
essentially a contract tort
even with God right there
in the tall reeds.

But no forgiveness, no reconciliation,
the human condition poised for perdition
here and here-after.

Monarchs, would-be Gods, exalted mimes,
drew up laundry lists of capital crimes,
hanging their dirty linen in the public square
blood-soaked, tear-stained, a hellish affair.

Our Puritan forebears, upright, uptight
looked for Satan, found him each night
making auditions and confirming suspicions
in the Wild Woods of the New World.

Their Salem Witch Hunt
mock trials, mock sins
pure Mischief even then
set the Gold Standard for revenge,
one we've revisited time and again,
most recently with Demon Rum and
Drugs in the Slum, and pretty nearly every
Raisin in the Sun.

Here's a simple history lesson,
we can do better than repression
which bars people
from the light of day
excludes them from our way

Prison makes the metaphor real
a matter of concrete and steel.
Reification and, over time,
a prison nation.

Poetic justice, then,
amounts to this:
Sanctions that harden
started in the Garden
We were Beaten in Eden
rooted out like weeds
hence the seeds
of discontent
spread so widely
hence the flowers
of forgiveness
spread so thin.

Which raises a question,
in the inquiring mind,
Is it the punishment
or is it the crime
fueling the resentments
Of our time?

Is it crime and punishment
that go hand in hand?
Or does punishment feed the crime
that plagues our land?

Reconciliation or revenge?
On this choice
Our future
May hinge.

Addendum: Domestic Justice

Dead Girls on Stage

"Would there ever be dead girls on stage?"
The question drifted up from the back of the car,
in the lilting cadence of my then five year old son, Brian,
transfixed by the bright, flashing neon sign,
"LIVE GIRLS ON STAGE"
and, below that, "NO COVER."

I laughed, awed by the beauty
and nuance of language, and
maybe a fleeting image of young,
exotic dancers in the flesh.
"No Cover."

"The girls are physically alive," I said.
"Grown men (like Daddy?) pay
to look at their bodies,
to watch them dance."

At my wife's raised eyebrow, I added, lamely,
"Some people consider stripping an art form,
like ballet."

Silence.

"Okay, mostly it's a bad thing.
The work gets old and the men get older.
The girls get drunk and the men get drunker.
There's groping and grabbing, mean talk.
After hours, you've got fights and rapes and arrests.
It's a life that crushes dignity, slow but sure."

"Would there ever be dead girls on stage?"
Absolutely, all the time.

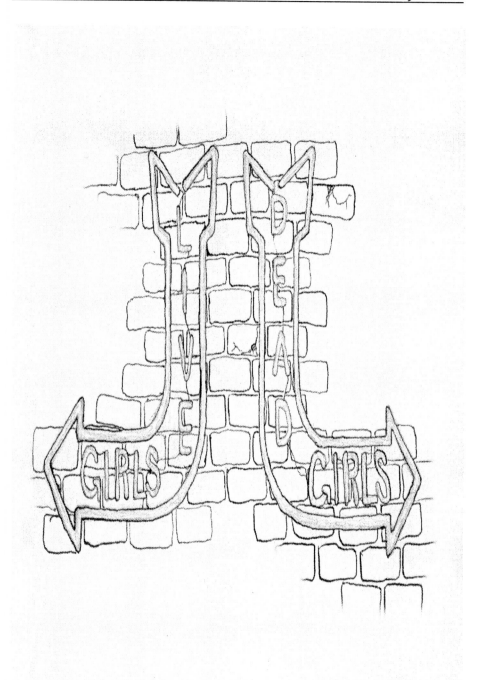

Eleanor Potter

Secret Circus, At Your Service

"You've got a call from the Secret Circus,"
the message read, in the unmistakable
scrawl of my son, Patrick, then a first-grader.

I thought of men in dark coats and dark suits, discrete
cover for colorful clown costumes.
Their disguise as Secret Service Agents
would be diabolically effective, I mused,
except perhaps for the shoes.
How would you hide those big clown shoes?
Not even wingtips have the wingspan
for that cover-up job.

"We're here from the Secret Circus,"
I imagined an agent saying, as he
took off his coat, loosened his staid tie,
and unbuttoned his vest and Brooks Brothers shirt
revealing a candy-stripped silk blouse
its fluffy accordion neck liner neatly tucked down,
now flipped upright and in full view.

As he carefully secured his bulbous red nose
to his handsome young face, he'd say,
in a dignified baritone, "It's a dangerous world out there.
Sometimes it's only us between you and the animals."

The thin red line, with stripes and polka dots,
manned by a thousand clowns,
folks ready to take the fall for us all,
and keep on smiling.

Eleanor Potter

Cooking with Kafka

"Cooking with Kafka," my wife said,
brightly, when asked what she
was doing that night, alone
in our kitchen, a few days
before Thanksgiving, amid pots
and pans and assorted
animal and plant detritus.

Kafka, I thought, pausing to reflect.
I was ready for banter, not discourse.
Who cooks with Kafka?
As it happens, she meant Barbara, not Franz,
he of lazy eye and diligent mind,
Poster Child for Existentialism,
Icon of Modern Alienation,
Oracle of Occult Organizational Forms,
of Surreal Trials and Peculiar Punishments.

No chef fit to wear an apron could picture
Franz Kakfa on the cover of a cookbook
or associate him with *any* menu plan,
let alone a *holiday* menu plan.
But I'm no cook, so my wife's off-hand comment
filled my head with images of existential feasts,
complete with bureaucratic schedules and lists,
seating plans secret and shifting,
food emblazoned with moral messages, carved
resolutely but lovingly into yielding animal flesh,
desserts of moral weight, served with ceremony,

Even a few guests behaving like cockroaches
greedily scouring their plates, always
with one eye (antennae?) on the next course.
Don't we all have guests now and again
who seem to metamorphose into cockroaches?
or at least behave like voracious insects?

Our holiday meals would be a trial,
I sensed, followed inevitably by the conviction
that we all deserve the punishment

we are inflicting on ourselves,
by cooking too much
and eating too much,
as we drive blindly down
the culinary cul-de-sac
reserved for Americans,

starting briskly with Thanksgiving turkey,
losing a step or two as holiday parties take their toll,
then lumbering (or waddling) on to Christmas ham,
bravely, with miles and miles of
stuffings and sweets to eat
before we lay us down to sleep,
heavily. Very heavily.

About the Author and Artists

Robert Johnson is the author of several social science books dealing with crime and punishment, including *Death Work: A Study of the Modern Execution Process*, winner of the Outstanding Book Award of the Academy of Criminal Justice Sciences. Many of the poems in this collection, Johnson's first, are drawn from his research in criminology. Robert Johnson is a Professor of Justice, Law and Society at American University in Washington, D.C.

Jennifer Leigh Adger received a B.S. in Psychology from Auburn University and a M.P.P. from Harvard University's John F. Kennedy School of Government. She is a doctoral student in Justice, Law and Society at American University, where she is pursuing her long-standing interest in crime and punishment, particularly the death penalty. Jen is also an artist, whose paintings have been sold over the Internet and at art shows.

Amy Hendrick received her B.A. from American University in 2002 with a major in Visual Media and a minor in Justice. While at American University, she was a teaching assistant responsible for various photography and visual media courses as well as an intern with the Metropolitan Police Department's Force Investigation Team. Amy is currently the President of Facilitating Leadership in Youth (F.L.Y.), a non-profit organization that works with youth in Washington, DC.

Eleanor Potter is studying for her BA in Fine Art at the University of Wales in Aberystwyth. A British citizen, she has lived in the Washington D.C. area for the past ten years. After graduating with the International Baccalaureate from the Washington International School, Eleanor completed her art foundation course at the Wimbledon School of Art in London, U.K. She has had her work displayed at the Goethe Institute in Washington D.C. as well as at exhibitions in the London area.

If Your enjoyed this poetry from the Poet's Press, you might enjoy some of our other recent releases.

Other poetry titles by the Poet's Press
(all in paperback unless noted)

Additional copies of this book *(Poetic Justice)*	18.95
CD, of author reading this book	13.95
Both	19.95
Hog Killers and other Poems by Vernon Schmid	12.95
If ordered with one of above, only	9.95
Aesop's Eagles and Poems from the Road	
By Anne Harding Woodworth	12.95
CD, Author reads the book	13.95
Both	19.95
The Mushroom Papers	
By Anne Harding Woodworth	12.95
CD, selected poems from book, Author reads	13.95
Between the Faces of Janus By Paul Felsch, III	12.95
CD, author reads	13.95
Both	19.95
What Rough Beast by S. M. Hall, III	12.95
CD author reading	13.95
Both	19.95
Michelangelo's Call by Sy Hakim	12.95
Only This, by Roy Schwartzman	12.95
CD, author reads	13.95
Both	19.95

Shipping, $3.25 for first copy, plus .65 for ea additional to same address
Books going to Maine must include 5% sales tax.
Order from

Order Department
PO Box 298
Thomaston Maine 04861